7/16

Sheriffs and Deputies

by Meish Goldish

Consultant: Jan Caldwell
Media Relations Director
San Diego County Sheriff's Department
San Diego, California

BEARPORT
PUBLISHING

New York, New York

Credits

Cover and Title Page, © Rudy Umans/Shutterstock, © Bikeriderlondon/Shutterstock, and © Blend Images/Shutterstock; 4–5, © bikeriderlondon/Shutterstock; 5 Inset, © Sam Smith; 6, © Eldad Carin/Shutterstock; 6 Background, © Planner/Shutterstock; 7, © Courtesy of The Union-Recorder; 8, © RON T. ENNIS/KRT/Newscom; 9L, © ZUMA Press, Inc/Alamy; 9R, © TFoxFoto/Shutterstock; 10, © Courtesy of Rose Palmisano, The Orange County Register; 11, © Blaylock/The Augusta Chronicle; 12–13, © Stuart Palley/ZUMA Press/Corbis; 13, © bikeriderlondon/Shutterstock; 14, © Fresno County Sheriff's Search & Rescue Team; 15, © Fresno County Sheriff's Search & Rescue Team; 16–17, © marchello74/Shutterstock; 17R, © Greg Hume/Wikipedia; 18, © Tyler Olson/Shutterstock; 19, © Courtesy of the Gainesville Sun; 20, © hans engbers/Shutterstock; 21T, © Courtesy of the Hillsborough County Sheriff Department; 21B, © Steve Byland/Shutterstock; 22, © Don Graham; 23, © MICHAEL REYNOLDS/EPA/Newscom; 24, © Dallas Oregon Fire & EMS; 25, © Dallas Oregon Fire & EMS; 26, © Courtesy of Brittany Fraser/Brick Animal Rescue; 27, © Courtesy of the Porter County Sheriff's Office; 28T, © Niteshift36/Wikimedia; 28BL, © Gregory Bull/AP/Corbis; 28BR, © davidsansegundo/Shutterstock; 29T, © JASON REDMOND/REUTERS/Newscom; 29M, © Vladimir L./Shutterstock.

Publisher: Kenn Goin
Editor: Jessica Rudolph
Creative Director: Spencer Brinker
Design: Dawn Beard Creative
Photo Researcher: We Research Pictures, LLC.

Library of Congress Cataloging-in-Publication Data in process at time of publication (2016)
Library of Congress Control Number: 2015039375
ISBN-13: 978-1-943553-16-7

Copyright © 2016 Bearport Publishing Company, Inc. All rights reserved. No part of this publication may be reproduced in whole or in part, stored in any retrieval system, or transmitted in any form or by any means, electronic, mechanical, photocopying, recording, or otherwise, without written permission from the publisher.

For more information, write to Bearport Publishing Company, Inc., 45 West 21st Street, Suite 3B, New York, New York 10010. Printed in the United States of America.

10 9 8 7 6 5 4 3 2 1

Contents

Trapped in a Fire!

One afternoon in December 2014, Deputy Josh Mays got a call that someone at a house in Baldwin **County**, Georgia, might be in trouble. When the deputy drove to the address, he found the house **engulfed** in fire. Flames crawled up the walls and roof, and thick smoke poured out of the windows. Deputy Mays reported the fire to the **dispatcher** and then checked inside the home. That's when he heard Patsy Smith screaming for help.

The dispatcher had received a 9-1-1 call from Patsy, but the call got cut off before she could say anything. Concerned, the dispatcher **traced** the call to Patsy's address and sent Deputy Mays to check things out.

At first, the smoke was so thick that Deputy Mays couldn't see Patsy. Finally, he spotted her behind a kitchen table. Mays tried three times to reach the **victim**. Each time, the heavy smoke drove him back. Even worse, the roof was starting to cave in. The deputy had to act fast, but what could he do?

Deputy Mays arrived at the scene of the fire in a vehicle like this one.

Facing the Flames

Soon, a second deputy arrived at the house with gas masks. Deputy Mays put a mask on and raced into the smoke-filled kitchen. He grabbed Patsy and quickly pulled her out of the house. The victim was badly burned. However, thanks to the deputy's brave rescue, she survived the terrible blaze.

Gas masks prevent people from breathing in harmful gases during a fire, and protect the eyes from smoke and soot.

After the rescue, Baldwin County Sheriff Bill Massee praised his deputy. "I am extremely proud of Deputy Mays," he said. "I'm not surprised that he would confront a fire to save a life. He is a person who was not going to let someone die."

Deputy Mays (center) and other members of the Baldwin County Sheriff's Department received awards for helping to save Patsy Smith.

What Are Sheriffs and Deputies?

Sheriff's Departments are law enforcement organizations found in counties across the United States. In a Sheriff's Department, one sheriff oversees many deputies. The deputies do the same type of work as police officers. However, deputies **enforce** the law in areas of a county outside of cities and towns that have their own police departments. Sometimes, this means deputies work in **rural** places, such as farming communities.

Deputies **patrol** neighborhoods, **investigate** crimes, and make arrests. They also do important search-and-rescue work. Deputies look for missing people and rescue victims of car accidents, fires, and other disasters.

This deputy was lowered from a helicopter so he could rescue a fourteen-year-old boy trapped in a river.

 Many Sheriff's Departments have a search-and-rescue team made up of **volunteers**. The volunteers do not have all the duties of a deputy, but they are specially trained to find and save missing people.

Deputies investigating a car crash

9

Job Training

Before they can become deputies, **recruits** have to train at a law enforcement **academy**. They must pass tough physical tests, such as running several miles and lifting heavy weights. They also have to complete an **obstacle course** where they climb walls and crawl through small spaces. These activities prepare the **trainees** for difficult real-life rescues.

Trainees running at an academy

Deputy trainees are also taught many important skills. They learn to drive fast but safely, so they can rush to the scene of an emergency without putting other drivers at risk. They are taught how to give **first aid** to someone who is sick or injured. Trainees also learn how to control large crowds and how to defend themselves if attacked.

Trainees learn how to give emergency care to victims by practicing on dummies.

During first-aid training, deputies learn how to treat broken bones, burns, and other wounds. They also learn how to give **CPR** to a person who has stopped breathing.

Lost on a Mountain

Tough training can prepare deputies for search-and-rescue work in dangerous areas—even at the top of a mountain. In July 2012, Lawrence Bishop was hiking with friends in California's Sierra National Forest when he left his group to climb a 2-mile-high (3.2 km) mountain by himself. After reaching the top, he chose a path back down the mountain that was extremely **steep** and slippery.

Sierra National Forest

On the way down, Lawrence fell and then slid down a rocky slope. He ended up on a narrow **ledge** just a few inches wide, his body covered in cuts. He struggled to stay balanced on the ledge. Lawrence realized he was trapped and had to wait for help to arrive.

When darkness came, Lawrence forced himself to stay awake, afraid he would fall if he slept. Friends reported him missing the next day, and members of the Fresno County Sheriff's Office Search and Rescue Team began looking for him.

With no food or water, Lawrence grew very dizzy. He was so certain he was going to fall off the mountain and die that he wrote a good-bye letter to his wife and daughter.

Lawrence didn't have any food, water, or other survival supplies that hikers should carry in case they get lost on a mountain.

Racing up the Peak

For the next 24 hours, deputies looked for Lawrence in the mountains. By his third day on the ledge, the **stranded** hiker was so tired and weak that his body started to tremble. That's when he saw a group of rescuers hiking up the mountain. Lawrence cried out, "Help me!"

Fortunately, Deputy David Rippe heard the hiker shouting. The deputy saw that Lawrence "looked like he was just about ready to fall." So, Deputy Rippe raced 100 yards (91.4 m) up the smooth, rocky cliff—with no climbing ropes to aid him.

Deputy Rippe

Lawrence

The deputy grabbed Lawrence just in time. Soon, a police helicopter arrived on the scene and lowered a rope to the men. Deputy Rippe secured the rope to the hiker, and the two were lifted to safety. Lawrence is extremely grateful to the deputy. "He saved my life."

A helicopter hovers over Deputy Rippe and Lawrence.

Lawrence couldn't believe Deputy Rippe ran up the steep, slippery mountain with no climbing ropes. "This guy would put mountain goats to shame!" said Lawrence.

Runaway Dog

Deputies don't just rescue people. Sometimes they help animals, too. One morning in Florida in 2010, Melisse Moehlig was walking her dog, Layla, when a car suddenly hit both of them. Melisse was sent flying 60 feet (18 m) into the air. Layla was dragged 80 feet (24 m) before the driver finally stopped the car. One of the dog's legs was trapped under a tire.

Layla is a type of dog called a black mouth cur.

Luckily, Alachua County Sheriff's Department Deputies Kevin Davis and Kathy Zedalis were on patrol nearby and saw the accident. Deputy Zedalis called an ambulance, and raced to treat Melisse's injuries. Meanwhile, Deputy Davis pulled the driver out of the car. Then, he got into the vehicle and drove it off Layla's leg. The dog, bleeding heavily and yelping in pain, got up and ran away.

Deputies keep a first-aid kit in their patrol car so they can provide emergency medical help while waiting for an ambulance to arrive.

Helping Layla

Soon, an ambulance arrived, and paramedics rushed Melisse to the hospital. She had broken bones in her right shoulder and left leg. Despite her own pain, she was more concerned about Layla. So, Deputy Davis went to look for the dog. He drove to Melisse's home and found the **canine** lying near the front door. Layla's back right leg was still bleeding heavily, and most of the skin around it was stripped away.

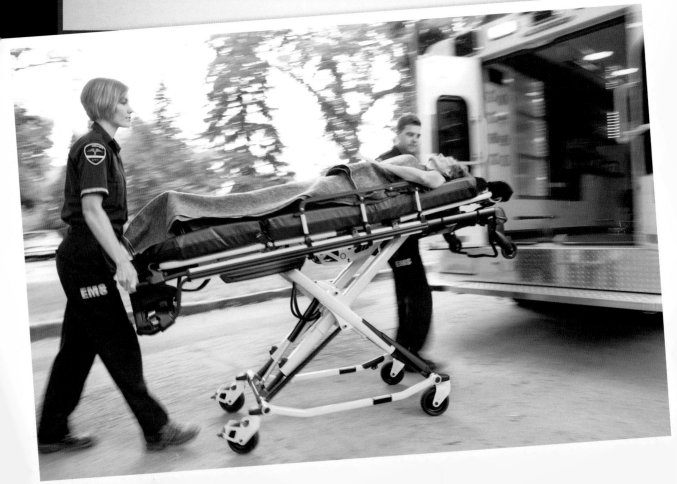

Deputy Davis used a first-aid kit to stop the bleeding. Then he took the dog to an animal hospital, where Layla's badly injured leg had to be **amputated**. Within days, though, Layla was home, learning how to walk on three legs. Melisse also recovered and is happy to have her dog back. "I am so appreciative of everything the deputies did for us," she says.

After Layla healed from her operation, Deputy Davis visited her.

Deputy Davis used QuikClot® on Layla's leg. This product was developed by the army to save lives on the battlefield. It quickly causes blood to **clot** so wounds stop bleeding.

Working Together

Although deputies are highly skilled, they cannot always perform rescues alone. Sometimes they need help from other emergency responders. In March 2014, a man in Florida saw a huge bull stuck in a pond. The animal was struggling to keep its head above water. The man called the Hillsborough County Sheriff's Office, which sent Deputy Christina Ammons and her partner to investigate.

Bulls and cows can be very large. The bull that got stuck in the pond weighed 1,000 pounds (454 kg)!

At the pond, Deputy Ammons took off her gun belt and uniform shirt and **waded** into the water. She held the bull's head up so the animal wouldn't drown. Soon, firefighters arrived to help. They placed **tow straps** around the heavy bull and dragged it onto land. With the deputies and firefighters working together, the animal managed to walk away unhurt.

Deputy Ammons (left) held the bull's head up for 45 minutes until firefighters arrived and pulled the animal onto shore with tow straps.

 While Deputy Ammons helped the bull, her partner held a rifle and watched for alligators that might try to attack! Alligators are a common sight in many parts of Florida.

A Hero's Reward

Sometimes, deputies **respond** to emergencies even when they are off-duty. In April 2013, Deputy Jenna Underwood-Nunez of the Los Angeles County Sheriff's Department was camping with her family near a lake. Suddenly, she heard a child shouting. She looked toward the lake and saw a boy in the water, about 100 yards (91.4 m) from shore. The deputy—who was five months pregnant—immediately jumped into the water and swam out to the boy.

Deputy Underwood-Nunez was camping at Silverwood Lake in Southern California.

When she reached him, the boy told Deputy Underwood-Nunez that his 17-year-old brother was under the water, drowning. The deputy dove deep into the muddy water. She found the victim about 15 feet (4.6 m) below the surface, grabbed him, and started swimming. When she got him back to shore, he wasn't breathing. She performed CPR until he started to breathe on his own again. Thanks to Deputy Underwood-Nunez's heroic rescue, the teen made a full recovery.

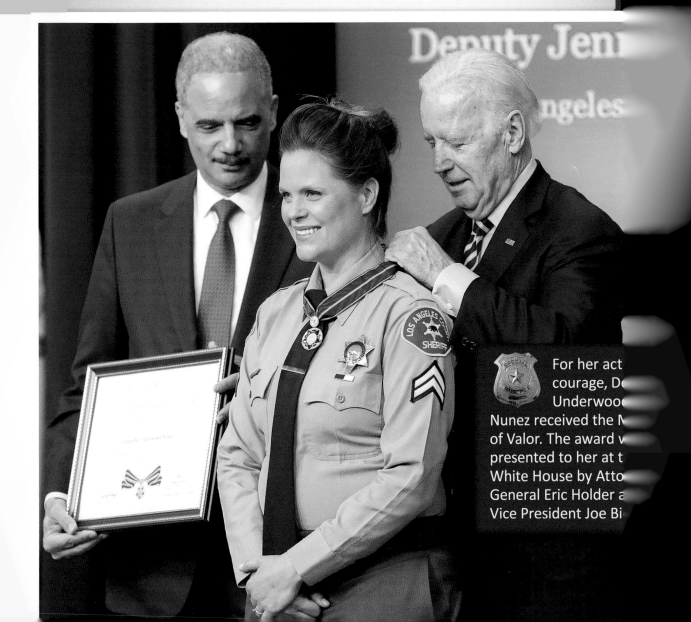

For her act
courage, De
Underwood
Nunez received the M
of Valor. The award v
presented to her at t
White House by Atto
General Eric Holder a
Vice President Joe Bi

Rescuing the Rescuer

Sometimes deputies must work together with other law enforcement personnel to save one of their own. That's what happened one afternoon in Texas in July 2015. Polk County Sheriff's Deputy Shon Latty was responding to an emergency call. As he sped to the scene, a pickup truck slammed into the deputy's patrol car. The car went flying into a ditch and caught fire. Deputy Latty suffered a broken arm and shoulder, and was too injured to move. He was trapped inside the burning car!

Car fires are extremely dangerous. The gasoline in the car's tank is at risk of exploding, and anyone nearby could be injured or even killed.

Luckily, another deputy and two Dallas police officers arrived within minutes to help. The deputy and one of the officers used **fire extinguishers** to battle the flames. The other officer tried to free Deputy Latty. It was difficult work. Because the front of the patrol car was crushed, Deputy Latty's legs were pinned to his seat. Eventually, the officer was able to pull him out of the car. Thanks to the fast actions of the deputy and the cops, Deputy Latty was safe.

Officer Colby Hamilton, who helped save Deputy Latty, said, "We put our lives on

Dedicated to the Job

It takes a special kind of person to work in a Sheriff's Department. Brittany Fraser works as a deputy for the Los Angeles County Sheriff's Department. She's always ready to help, no matter who the victim is. Part of her job includes rescuing lost, injured, and **stray** animals. "As much as I want to help people, it's the same for animals," says Deputy Fraser.

In Washington State, Okanogan County Sheriff Frank Rogers says, "We all get into law enforcement because we truly want to help." He calls being a Sheriff "the greatest job in the world." Thanks to **dedicated** workers like Sheriff Rogers and Deputy Fraser, anyone in need of a rescue can rely on the local Sheriff's Department.

Many sheriffs and

Sheriffs' and Deputies' Equipment

Sheriffs and deputies use special equipment when they're on the job. Here is some of their gear.

A *light bar* has flashing lights that can easily be seen so other drivers know to make room on the road for the vehicle.

SHERIFF
LEE COUNTY
7248

A *label* and *emblem* identify the car as belonging to the Sheriff's Department.

A *laptop computer* is used by the Sheriff or deputy to find information.

A *two-way radio* allows the Sheriff or deputy to stay in touch with other deputies.

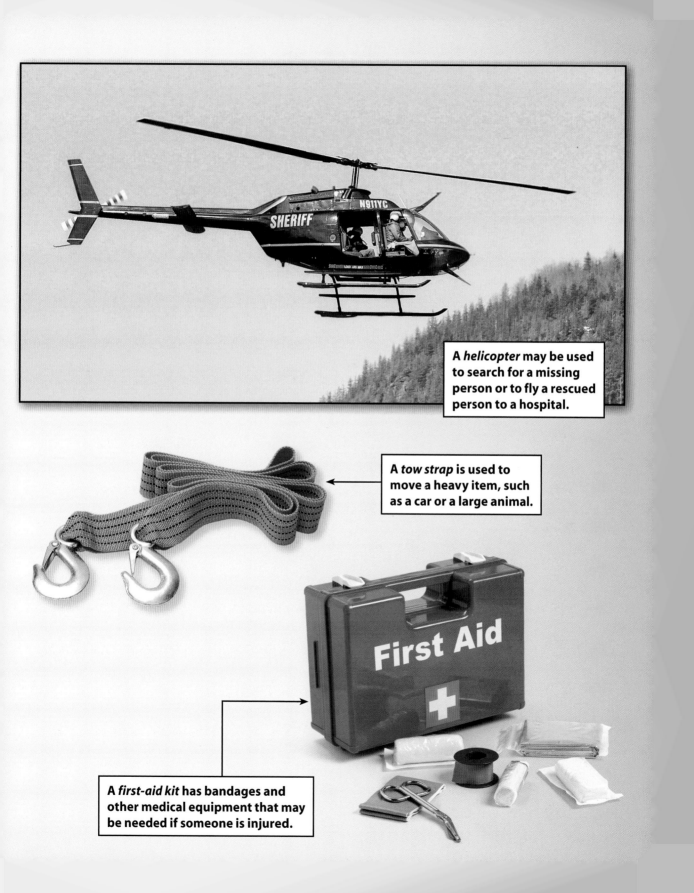

A *helicopter* may be used to search for a missing person or to fly a rescued person to a hospital.

A *tow strap* is used to move a heavy item, such as a car or a large animal.

A *first-aid kit* has bandages and other medical equipment that may be needed if someone is injured.

Glossary

academy (uh-KAD-uh-mee) a school that teaches special subjects or skills

amputated (AM-pyoo-*tay*-tid) cut off a body part for medical reasons

canine (KAY-nine) a dog

clot (KLAHT) to become thick; when blood clots it sticks together and stops flowing from an injury

county (KOUN-tee) a division or part of a state, with its own local government

CPR (SEE-PEE-AHR) letters stand for *cardiopulmonary resuscitation*; a type of rescue where a person blows air into the mouth and then presses down on the chest of someone whose heart has stopped

dedicated (DED-ih-*kay*-tid) devoted, loyal

dispatcher (diss-PATCH-ur) an operator who takes emergency calls and sends out people to help others

enforce (en-FORSS) to make sure that laws are obeyed

engulfed (en-GUHLFD) covered completely; overwhelmed

fire extinguishers (FYE-ur ek-STING-gwish-urz) devices that release streams of water, foam, or other chemicals to put out fires

first aid (FURST AYD) care given to an injured or sick person in an emergency before he or she is treated by a doctor

investigate (in-VESS-tuh-*gayt*) to search for information to find out about something

ledge (LEDJ) a narrow, rocky shelf on the side of a mountain

obstacle course (OB-stuh-kuhl KORSS) a training area that is filled with hurdles, fences, and walls that trainees must get over

patrol (puh-TROHL) to travel around an area to keep it safe

recruits (rih-KROOTS) people who have recently joined a group

respond (rih-SPOND) to arrive at the scene of an emergency to provide help

rural (RUR-uhl) having to do with the countryside; away from cities

steep (STEEP) having a sharp slope or slant

stranded (STRAN-did) left helpless in a strange or dangerous place

stray (STRAY) lost or homeless

tow straps (TOH STRAPS) strips of leather or nylon that are used to pull a heavy object

traced (TRAYSD) found or discovered by investigation

trainees (tray-NEEZ) people who are being taught particular work skills

victim (VIK-tuhm) a person who is hurt or killed

volunteers (vol-uhn-TIHRZ) people who help others for no pay

waded (WAY-did) walked through shallow water or mud

Bibliography

Marcum, Diana. "Hiker's Rescuer Sprints Up 300 Feet of Smooth Rock, Just in Time." *Los Angeles Times* (August 2, 2012).

Taylor, Krasne V. *Within the Walls: The Epitome of a Sheriff's Deputy.* Oak Park, MI: Ora's Publishing (2005).

Read More

Blake, Kevin. *Air-Sea Rescue Officers (Police: Search & Rescue!).* New York: Bearport (2016).

Goldish, Meish. *State Troopers (Police: Search & Rescue!).* New York: Bearport (2016).

Green, Michael. *Sheriffs and Deputy Sheriffs.* Mankato, MN: Capstone (1999).

White, Nancy. *Police Officers to the Rescue (The Work of Heroes: First Responders in Action).* New York: Bearport (2012).

Learn More Online

To learn more about sheriffs and deputies, visit
www.bearportpublishing.com/PoliceSearchAndRescue

Index

About the Author

Meish Goldish has written more than 200 books for children. His book *Animal Control Officers to the Rescue* was a Children's Choices Selection in 2014. He lives in Brooklyn, New York.